The
Presenter's
Edge

Third Edition

HOW TO UNLOCK YOUR INNER SPEAKER

Gavin Meikle

Design and layout: Charles Design Associates
Photography: Sandra Śnieżek (Chione Photography)

Cover photographs courtesy of Fotolia

At the time of going to press, all web addresses were active and contained
information relevant to the topics in this book. Gavin Meikle does not,
however, accept responsibility for the content or views contained on these
websites. Content, views and addresses may change beyond the publisher
or author's control.

Acknowledgements

Despite what the author may say, no book is ever entirely the creation of a single person. The ideas that go into it have inevitably been gathered from multiple sources over months or years. The style has been influenced by teachers, critics, colleagues, readers and reviewers. The format and layout have been influenced directly and indirectly by friends, colleagues, other authors, editors, etc. This book is no different;

To single out any one person seems inappropriate but there are a few people I really must thank as they have been instrumental in helping me through the process of writing this book.

Firstly, a huge thank you to my wonderful wife, Lyn, for her endless support and encouragement. Secondly to the members of *Solent Speakers*, my local *Toastmasters Club*, who have provided examples and support to me, as well as giving invaluable feedback. You have helped me grow and develop as a speaker and a leader.

To my reviewer panel, thank you for giving up your precious time to read the earlier drafts of this book and suggest improvements.

Finally, thanks to my wonderful clients, from whom I have learned so much.

Contents

Introduction

"The single biggest problem in communication is the illusion that it has taken place."

George Bernard Shaw

THE PROBLEM WITH PRESENTATIONS

Presentations should be a powerful and effective way to communicate, educate, influence and entertain but, in my experience, they rarely live up to this ideal.

I shudder at the thought of how many hours I have wasted sitting through pointless, poorly prepared and badly delivered presentations, and I think it's pretty safe to say that you have too. Now imagine multiplying that by the number of speeches and presentations that are delivered across the globe every day!

The most common reasons for this poor quality are:
- Missing or inappropriate outcomes
- Lack of relevant content
- Poor structure
- Dull delivery style
- Inappropriate use of visual aids

It doesn't have to be like this.

Follow the tips in this book and you can be part of a much-needed revolution to transform the way people around the world communicate.

Will you join me?

YOU CAN BECOME PART OF THE SOLUTION RATHER THAN THE PROBLEM

- Learn how to create presentations that instantly engage your audience
- Learn how to choose the right content for your audience's starting point
- Learn how to structure your content so that it is both persuasive and easy to follow
- Learn how to deliver that content in a style that is interesting, engaging and authentic.

My intention, when writing this book was to create a practicable, easy to read, 'how to' guide for presenters of all standards. A bite-sized book, that will give you rapid access to a range of proven presentation tools, techniques and tips.

WHAT'S IN IT FOR YOU?

Changing behaviour takes effort and commitment. Unless we have a good reason for doing something different, the odds are stacked in favour of our existing behaviour. So let's stop and take a moment to think about the personal and professional benefits that will come when you choose to become a better presenter.

Transform your terror

The techniques in this book will help turn what used to be an ordeal into an enjoyable experience. I can say this with confidence because I have seen it happen countless times.

It's a wonderful feeling to witness when someone realises that the beliefs they have held about themselves, were completely wrong. That feeling of awakening that comes when you realise that it is possible to enjoy speaking in front of an audience is life changing.

They all say that the buzz they get from engaging fully with their audience is amazing.

Boost your opportunities for promotion

Persuasive presentation skills are much in demand in every sector. If you don't believe me, just look at how many interviews include a short presentation. Savvy employers know that staff who can communicate with groups in a persuasive manner add real value to their business. In fact, I'd go so far as to say that it's virtually impossible to find a job now that doesn't require the candidate to have at least basic public speaking skills.

I got my first promotion directly as a result of a presentation I gave after having been involved in a market research project. That presentation got me noticed and promotion came shortly afterwards. Just ask around and I'm sure you'll hear lots of similar stories.

Boost your ability to influence others

Whether you are an employee or a business owner you'll need to influence others, be they colleagues, customers or suppliers. Use the skills explained in this book and you will become more persuasive. Think how good it will feel when your voice is heard and acknowledged.

Be a role model for others

Becoming a confident presenter benefits others as well. When you speak well, you set a positive example for your colleagues, customers and kids. When others see an engaging and articulate speaker they are inspired to learn how to do so too. If you want your staff to be better communicators you need to set them a positive example.

WHAT TOPICS DOES THIS BOOK COVER?

Effective public speaking and presenting is a BIG subject so I have chosen to cover the key elements in some depth. In this book you will learn more about the three key elements of any presentation.

Content + Structure + Delivery

Specifically, I'll cover:

- Tips for overcoming your fear of public speaking
- How to set a specific presentation purpose
- How to establish audience relevance
- The value of the 'Backwards Planning' technique
- Structuring your presentation for maximum effect
- Intelligent visual aid design and usage

- The importance of the 'walk-on'
- Using eye contact to engage your audience
- How to stand and move when 'on stage'
- What to do with your hands when you are speaking
- How to use the power of the pause
- The most time efficient way to rehearse your speech
- The value of getting specific, constructive feedback
- How to prepare for and handle audience questions.

KEY TERMS USED IN THIS BOOK

Audience

I use the term audience to denote the people who are listening to your presentation or speech. Depending on your profession, these could include, students, jurors, customers, co-workers or employees.

Presentation

In this book I use the term 'presentation' in it's most general sense to encompass formal speeches, informal talks and persuasive presentations.

HOW TO GET THE MOST OUT OF THIS BOOK

There is no 'right way' to read this book. How you use it will depend on your reading preferences, your desired outcomes and your current level of speaking skills.

Novice speakers will typically start by reading it through from cover to cover, whilst more experienced speakers may prefer to dip into specific sections. Whichever approach you choose, the most important thing is that you practice the techniques!

To help you I have included numerous links to the web pages supporting this book. There you'll find video clips, articles and downloadable resources to help you.

As well as links that you can cut and paste into your browser, I have included QR codes that, when scanned using a phone or tablet, will take you straight to the web page.

NOTE: Depending on your device you may need to download a QR Code reader app. There are many free ones available for Android and iOS devices.

Chapter 1 – Foundations for Success

THREE KEYS TO SPEAKING SUCCESS

If you are to become adept at developing and delivering effective, entertaining and engaging presentations there are three skill areas that you will need to master.

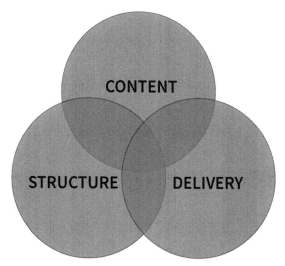

Content

By content I mean the information, ideas and evidence that you present to your audience during your talk.

- Data – Facts, figures, statistics
- Anecdotes and metaphors
- Case studies & examples
- Reasons and explanations
- Problems and solutions
- Benefits & consequences.

The content you include should depend on a number of factors including:

- The purpose of your presentation
- The nature & composition of your audience

- Your knowledge of the subject
- The time available

When people have to give a presentation, they tend to spend the greater part of their preparation working on the content. Clearly it is important, but remember, content on its own is no guarantee of success. If your content is poorly organised and/or poorly delivered, your audience will quickly 'switch off' and all that effort will have been wasted. We'll go into speech content in more depth in one of the later chapters.

Structure

The organisation of your content is also a critical factor in the success of your presentation or speech. Like a good meal, every speech needs the following 3 elements:

- An attention grabbing opening (the appetiser)
- A body (the main course)
- A strong, memorable conclusion (the dessert)

We'll look at each of these elements in much more detail later along with handy techniques signpost the transitions from one section to another. A poorly structured presentation is difficult to follow and usually leads to confusion and/or boredom in your audience.

Neither of these are desirable if you really want to educate, influence or entertain.

Delivery

Last in our triad of skills, but by no means least, is the way you use your voice and body to deliver your presentation to your audience. Your delivery is absolutely critical to the success of your presentation but many people give it little, if any, thought to:

- Eye contact
- Stance, gestures and movement
- Facial expression
- Voice (volume, speed, tone, intonation, pauses)

I'm sure you have experienced how poor delivery skills can kill even the best scripted content. We'll cover these in detail in chapters 7, 8 and 9.

COMMON PRESENTATION MYTHS DEBUNKED

Goods speakers are born not made

Many people mistakenly believe that the ability to speak in public is a genetic trait. Something that you are born with. The truth is that the best speakers practice their delivery over and over again until it becomes second nature. They also seek out constructive feedback from their peers so that they can build upon their existing skills and address any bad habits.

Public speaking is a skill that anybody can master with practice. I know because I have seen many people who could hardly string two words together when standing in front of an audience become competent speakers in a few short months. That's the power of the techniques in this book.

Only extroverts make good speakers

I hate to be the bearer of bad news, but this is simply not true. If you don't believe me, look at the example set by the late Steve Jobs, CEO of Apple. If you have ever seen him speak you'll know that he wasn't the stereotypical 'larger than life' presenter. Despite this he was still a very good speaker. (If you haven't seen him speak, you can find lots of examples of his presentations on YouTube.) Anyone can be a good speaker. The key is to find your own authentic style.

> *"Be the best version of yourself you can be."*

It's all about the presenter

In truth, it's the audience who are the most important people in the room during your presentation. Your job as the presenter is to create a shift in your audience members' attitudes from where it is at the start of your speech, to where you need it to be, for them to do what you want them to do.

CHAPTER 1 SUMMARY

A great presentation needs three things:
- Well prepared content that is immediately and obviously relevant to the audience and that appeals to both the logical and emotional sides of our brains
- A clear, logical, easy to follow structure with an attention grabbing opening, a compelling case and a powerful conclusion
- An engaging, authentic delivery style that grabs the audience's attention and holds it throughout the presentation

Public speaking is a learnable skill that anyone can master with practice and guidance

Chapter 2 – Consider your Content

"Success depends on previous preparation, and without such preparation there is sure to be failure."

Confuscius

WHAT IS CONTENT?

In a nutshell, content is the information you present to your audience, and it comes in many forms including:

- Data – facts, figures, statistics
- Anecdotes and metaphors
- Case studies & examples
- Reasons & explanations
- Problems & solutions
- Benefits & consequences

This is where many people start, but it may surprise you to know that is shouldn't be:

> *"The content you include should depend on who you are speaking to and what you want to achieve."*

Spending time answering these two questions will ensure that your presentation is much more likely to be successful.

START WITH THE END IN MIND

- What is the purpose of your presentation?
- What do you want your audience to do?

Having sat through way too many bad presentations it became evident to me that most presenters have survival as their primary outcome! They just want to fill a slot of time without making a fool of themselves. While this is understandable, it probably explains why so many presentations are dull, boring and irrelevant.

What would happen if you focused on your audience rather than yourself?

If it is a sales presentation, for example, I presume that you want the customer to say "Yes" to your proposal or to agree to a trial of your services.

If it is an educational presentation, you might start by wanting your audience to be saying "I've got it!"or "Now I understand," but is that enough?

On one of my courses I asked the students to give me an example of a presentation outcome.

One delegate said, " I want them to understand."

I then asked her, "If they understand what you are saying but are not motivated to do something after you presentation would you be satisfied?"

Her answer was No!

A better outcome would be to identify what you want the audience members to do as a result of that learning.

If it is a briefing presentation, most likely you want your audience to understand and be sufficiently motivated to share the information with their team or customers.

If your purpose is primarily entertainment, such as an after dinner speech, I assume you want the audience to be entertained, enthusiastic and to give you a warm round of applause.

Whatever your purpose, it pays to be clear about it **before** you start to consider what it is that you are going to say.

CONSIDER YOUR AUDIENCE!

Once you are clear about your outcome, you must set aside some time to think about your audience.

- Who are they?
- How much do they know already?
- What is their attitude towards your topic?
- What are their desires and expectations?
- What are their fears and concerns?

Make time for research

It is all too easy to assume that you know who your audiences are and what they want, but this is a risky strategy. Instead of relying on your assumptions, why not test them out by doing a bit of research to discover the truth?

- Ask for a list of likely attendees in advance
- Ask your colleagues if they know them
- If you know some of them, why not approach them in advance and ask them to help by answering a few simple questions
- Consider surveying your audience in advance

Establish the relevance up front

If you would like to make your presentations more effective and engaging, make sure that you help your audience to see the relevance of it for them before they switch off.

When I was a sales manager I used to attend the company's annual sales conference. At some point during the event, we would be 'subjected' to a compulsory presentation by Human Resources about the pension scheme.

Due to age range of the sales force, 80–90% of those in the room would switch off as soon as those presentations were announced. They felt they were too young, and that the subject was not relevant to them. Then one year something shocking happened.

We had a new presenter who clearly understood the need to engage the audience and to transform a potentially dull subject into something important.

He started by switching off the PowerPoint, turning up the house lights and coming out from behind the lectern to talk to us from the centre of the stage. This was different, and we all started to get curious.

Then he asked us to shout out what we wanted to do when we eventually retired. The energy in the room grew as people shared their dreams and aspirations.

Next, he paused, congratulated everyone on their energy and enthusiasm, and said, "Wow, you are an interesting group of people. I've just got one more question for you: how are you going to afford to do all those things when you no longer have a salary coming in?"

He paused again, allowing his question to hit home, and the result was an almost audible gulp. Then he said, "Because that is what pensions are for..."

He had transformed a potentially dull presentation on pensions into a genuinely relevant one about achieving our personal life goals.

From that moment on I decided to ensure that I always established the relevance of my talks to the audience up front. I wanted them to be in no doubt why they should stay awake and pay attention.

So, now that we know who our audience are, what we want them to do, and what's in it for them, we can start to plan how we are going to get them to want to do it. To help you do this I would like to share a powerful four step process that I call "Backwards Planning."

It is called backwards planning because it starts with the outcome i.e. what you want to happen as a result of your presentation. Once you know what this is, you can work backwards from it to decide what you will need to include in your presentation.

Since we want to move our audience towards a specific action, it makes sense that we should spend a moment thinking about what really drives all human behaviours.

A little psychology

The backwards planning process is based on an understanding of how human beings operate. Psychological research suggests that our behaviours are driven primarily by our feelings, which are in turn driven by our thoughts.

THINK ...FEEL ...DO

Let's forget our audience for a moment and go back to our own thoughts and feelings as a speaker.

If you were a nervous presenter and I told you that you had to give a presentation to a group of senior people what thoughts might run through YOUR head?

From talking to many reluctant presenters I know that this 'internal dialogue' often goes along the lines of – "Oh no! I hate presenting. I'll probably dry up and make a fool of myself. This is going to be a disaster."

Now consider the feelings that would arise as a result of these thoughts.

Fear, panic, and anxiety are all inevitable consequences of this sort of thinking.

Finally, imagine the physical behaviours that these emotions would produce; sweating; fidgeting; rapid heart rate; dry mouth; hesitant speech?

These physiological responses are unlikely to help you deliver a an engaging presentation are they? The results of delivering a presentation in this 'state' are liable to be disappointing to say the least.

But how does this apply to my audience?

The 'think, feel, do model' applies equally to your audience. You can use it, in reverse, to work out what to put into your presentation to generate your desired audience response!

> ### Step 1
> What do you want your audience to **do** as a result of your communication?

> ### Step 2
> What emotions do you think your audience will need to **feel** in order to do what you want them to do in Step 1?

> ### Step 3
> What will your audience need to be **think** in order to feel the emotions you have listed in Step 2?

> ### Step 4
> What content will you build into your communication to trigger your audience to think the thoughts you identified in Step 3?

Backwards planning in action – An example

1. What do you want your audience to do as a result of your presentation?

   For this example, let's say that you want your audience to be open to implementing a new system for handling customer complaints.

2. How will they need to feel in order to do this?

   My guess is that they will need to feel a little uneasy that their existing system is not up to the job. They will also need to feel confident that your proposed solution will deliver the desired results. They may also need to feel warm towards you as a potential solution supplier.

3. What will they need to think, to feel these feelings?

   In this example, they will need to be thinking things like:
   - *"The problem with our current system is bigger than I thought."*
   - *"Delaying a replacement is costing us a lot of money."*
   - *"These people clearly understand our business, and their solution seems to be proven to work in similar organisations."*

4. What could you say to get them to think this way?

   You will need to show them how much the problems with their existing system are costing them in terms of time, money and/or customer satisfaction. You'll also need to present case studies from similar customers which prove that your system works well and is reliable.

This approach requires a fundamental shift in thinking for many presenters because it places the focus firmly on the audience rather than the speaker. To help you develop this new way of thinking I have produced a simple backwards planning worksheet.

You can download it here:
https://goo.gl/cohN0S

A recent example of this was a photographer who wanted to encourage his audience to use a professional photograph in their social media profile.

He started his presentation by showing his audience a selection of poor profile pictures, he asked them to discuss what sort of first impression these pictures created.

Next, he showed them examples of excellent profile photos by way of comparison. Afterwards I heard lots of people talking about how they needed to update their own profile pictures and I know that many went on to book a professional photo shoot with the photographer who gave the presentation.

BRAINSTORM CONTENT IDEAS

Having got clear about your objectives and your audience, you can now start to brainstorm the potential content of your speech or presentation.

Doing a "brain dump" of all the key content ideas you might talk about is a great first step to creating a well thought out presentation or speech. Personally I favour mind mapping for this phase, but you may prefer to use a more traditional approach like outlining.

Another alternative is to jot down each content idea on a separate post-it note and then stick them on a wall or whiteboard.

Once you have done your initial list, sleep on it and then revisit it with a fresh eye to see if you have missed any key elements.

CHAPTER 2 SUMMARY

The two most important questions to ask when starting to prepare any presentation are:

- What do I want my audience to do next?

  If you don't know your destination, how can you even start to plan the journey?

- What's In It For Them?

  Successful presenters always put their audience first.

  They understand the importance of establishing the relevance of their content in the eyes of their audience.

Chapter 3 – Presentation Structure

If your presentation does not have a clear structure, your audience will find it hard to follow and, as a result, lose track and lose interest. The simplest and best model for most presentations is a simple three act structure.

ACT 1: THE OPENING

In this opening act, you need to answer five questions as you establish the context and relevance for your presentation.

Audience:
Who are your audience and what is their role in relation to the topic?

Context:
Where and when are your audience in relation to the subject you are speaking about?

Challenge:
What is the problem or challenge they are facing, to which this presentation relates?

Outcome:
- Where would the audience like to get to, in relation to this challenge?
- What is their desired future?

Solution:
- How are they are going to get there?
- What is your solution to their problem?

The above questions are adapted from the work of Cliff Atkinson as outlined in his excellent book 'Beyond Bullet Points' (Microsoft Press 2008).

Grab their attention

The way you start your presentation is critical. If you do not get your audience engaged quickly, then they will switch off, and you will have a hard job winning them back. Many presentations start with something mundane and boring such as the speaker's name and their credentials. Not the most attention-getting opening, wouldn't you agree?

Always start your presentation with a bang! You can You can introduce yourself once you have got them hooked. Here are some of the most powerful ways to engage your audience's attention.

1. Ask a question

Questions get your audience thinking and prime their mind for the messages to come. Obviously the question must be relevant to the topic of your presentation. Here are some examples to get you started.

- How important are the presentations you have to give?
- What would happen if we could speed up the handling of our customer complaints?
- What else would improve if we could be more confident?

2. Use a memorable quotation

A quotation can sometimes be a good way to arouse your audience's curiosity and get them thinking.

I often start a presentation on communication skills with the following quotation from Irish playwright George Bernard Shaw.

> *"The single biggest problem in communication is the illusion that it has taken place."*

You can find some great quotations on almost any topic with the help of a quick internet search.

3. Start with a shocking statistic

A relevant and surprising statistic can be an excellent way to stimulate your audience's interest.

For example:

"You can achieve a 30% increase in audience recall by implementing one small design tip in PowerPoint."

One statistic like this probably won't be enough to convince your audience on its own, but it will wake them up and arouse their curiosity.

4. Start with a story

Stories are intrinsically engaging and 'sticky' i.e. memorable. Before we developed writing, our ancestors would sit around the campfire and tell stories to pass on vital knowledge. Stories still play a vital part in communication today.

An example

Five years ago one of my students started their presentation with a story, and I still remember it as clearly as if it were yesterday.

"Imagine you are 14 years old and you live in a one-room mud-brick hut, in a little village in Nigeria. There are 30 other children in your village, and you have just four battered old, schoolbooks between you. A teacher visits the village school for only two hours, once a week. What are your chances of getting a reasonable education so that you can get a job and earn enough to support your family?"

5. Start with a challenge

Overtly challenging your audience to change their habits or their thoughts can be an effective way to gain their initial engagement.

After reading this book, I challenge you to change at least one thing about the way you present so that you can be more confident and persuasive.

For more information on the power of stories, I recommend that you read Chip and Dan Heath's great little paperback, 'Made to Stick' (Published by Arrow Books).

ACT 2: THE BODY

In this section, you need to provide the supporting arguments and evidence for the solution mentioned at the end of Act 1.

Many presenters equate content with facts and figures, assuming that pure logic is the key to persuasion. They overload their audience with an endless stream of numbers, graphs and charts assuming that more is better. In reality, nothing could be farther from the truth.

Human beings are inherently emotional creatures, and as we discovered earlier, our behaviours (including our decisions) are driven by our feelings.

Even the most analytical accountant has a heart and is at the mercy of their emotions but will rarely admit it.

To motivate our audience to approve, accept or implement our suggestions, we need to appeal to their emotional as well as logical minds.

So how do we do this?

Logical drivers

Use just enough relevant facts, figures and rational data to provide valid evidence for your case, without overloading your audience.

Emotional drivers

Use personalised case studies, stories and testimonials to turn dry, abstract data into real-life human examples that create an emotional response.

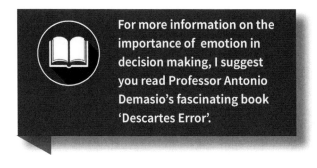

For more information on the importance of emotion in decision making, I suggest you read Professor Antonio Demasio's fascinating book 'Descartes Error'.

Divide your case into three main parts

The internal organisation of the content section is also vital. I recommend you organise your main content into no more than three sections each of which has its own key message. Each section can, in turn, be backed up by three supporting points.

Organising ideas into groups of three is a well-known and highly effective rhetorical device that has been used for thousands of years. Great orators from Plato to US President Barak Obama have used it because it makes it easier for the audience to digest and remember your key messages.

Transitions - the secret of a smoother flow

Presentations and speeches inevitably contain a range of different but related pieces of information, but the links between them may not be immediately obvious to the audience. Transitions are word bridges that help the audience to "join the dots" between the various ideas in your speech. A lack of transitions leads to a choppy, disjointed presentation that is too difficult to follow.

In a written document we use headings and sub headings to link different ideas together and to explain the relationship between different elements.

The best speakers achieve the same result in a verbal presentation through the use of speech transitions. These magical words and phrases smooth the transition between two ideas and reveal the relationship between the words you have just said and the words you are about to say.

The best way to understand what I mean by transitions is to consider the following examples:

Linking transitions

- In the same way...
- Another example of this is ....
- Similarly...

Contrastive transitions
- However...
- Others may feel that...
- On the other hand...

Elaborative transitions
- Additionally...
- In other words...
- Furthermore...

Illustrative transitions
- For example
- When we look at....
- We have all seen....

Sectional signposting
- So what can we do about this problem?...
- In conclusion...
- So let me summarise...

Handover transitions
- My colleague will now demonstrate...
- Now you are going to hear from.... who will...
- Our next speaker ...

ACT 3: THE CONCLUSION

Your conclusion is the last thing that your audience will hear so, if you want to leave them with a lasting positive impression, you'll need a strong conclusion!

Sadly many presenters neglect their conclusion and so their presentation just fades out or ends abruptly.

Your conclusion is the perfect place to repeat and reinforce your key messages and to make sure your audience knows what you want them to do next.

In my experience, this is most neglected part of most presentations. Many presentations end too abruptly without any advance warning and without any clear conclusion or definitive call to action.

If you want your audience to do something, use the conclusion to spell it out rather than assuming that they will just "get it".

Here are some examples of calls to action:

- Vote for me
- Select our proposal
- Go back and share this with your team

TOP TIP!

Rehearse your ending

Take the time to prepare a strong conclusion and then practice it sufficiently so that you know how you are going to finish.

CHAPTER 3 SUMMARY

A poorly organised or unstructured speech makes it hard for the listener to follow.

Make sure that your speech has an attention grabbing opening that establishes relevance and hooks their attention, giving them a reason to keep listening.

Don't forget the conclusion – it's the last thing that your audience hears, so it needs to be memorable and it ought to tell people what you want them to do next.

Remember to use transitional phrases to smooth the progression and explain the relationship between the different elements and ideas in your speech.

Chapter 4 – Writing Your Script

So, by now you should have an outcome, some ideas about your content and, an understanding of how best to organise and structure your presentation. Now it's time to sit down with a piece of paper or, more likely these days, a laptop, and start to create your presentation.

There is no "right way" to do this, but I want to share some top tips that I have learned from experimenting, reading and speaking to other presenters.

TOP TIP!
Don't start with PowerPoint
As will become apparent in the next chapter, visual aids should only be considered after you have drafted your speech script.

Don't start writing without a clear outcome
I know that I am repeating myself, but I do so for good reason. Beginning to write a presentation without a clear outcome is like trying to navigate in a wilderness without a compass.

Create an outline
I find it helpful to start with an overview and then to drill down and flesh out the details. I use mind mapping for this, but I know it does not suit everybody.
Effective alternatives include outlining or sticky notes.

Work to a target word count
As you may have noticed, good presenters tend to speak more slowly and deliberately than in normal conversation. Aim for a maximum speed of 120 words per minute. So, if you have a 20-minute slot for your presentation, your script should contain somewhere around 2,400 words.

Write with your audience in mind

As previously mentioned, your speech content should be aimed at a specific audience. Many presenters fail to tailor their content to suit their audience, resulting in a disappointing experience for both parties.

Take some time to think about the people you will be speaking to and choose your language, your data and your case studies with them in mind.

Write for the ear rather than the eye

Written communication is normally much more formal than spoken communication so sounds clunky and unnatural when read aloud.

To minimise this effect, imagine that you are speaking directly to the people in your audience, and then write down the words you would use in everyday speech. Contractions and colloquialisms such as "you'll" instead of "you will", are natural when speaking.

I know some speakers who use voice dictation software, such as 'Dragon Naturally Speaking', to help with this process.

Read your first draft out loud

This is an essential step as it will help you to eliminate overly formal language or tortuous tongue-tying phrases that will cause you to stumble. Revise any sections that don't sound 'right' or that are difficult to say.

Print it BIG

To make reading aloud easier and more natural, I recommend that you print out your script in a larger than normal font size, say 18 point.

TOP TIP!

Sleep on it before finalising

I have found that putting a speech to one side and then coming back to it with fresh eyes a day or two later makes a big difference. As well as giving yourself a break, it allows your brain to process unconsciously the ideas and messages, clarifying and simplifying them. The result is always a better speech or presentation.

Condense your script into a mind map or cue cards

Although it is technically possible to memorise a script word for word, it takes serious effort and it is rarely worth it.

Reading a script also makes it hard to maintain the eye contact and vocal variety necessary to keep your audience engaged.

Audiences are always impressed by speakers who can speak fluently without reading from their notes. Also, there is another problem with memorising a script word for word. If you stray from your script, your unconscious mind will notice and set off an alarm in your brain. This causes many inexperienced or nervous public speakers to panic.

The problem is that most people have not learned to trust their innate ability to say the right thing at the right time.

They prefer to write everything they are going to say on paper, or worse still, on their slides.

In truth, all you need are just a few prompt cards, containing enough keywords to trigger your memory and keep you on track. Many people find that 3" x 5" index cards work well as they are discreet and easy to handle.

Preventing cue card disaster
If you are using cue cards, always punch a **TOP TIP!** hole in the top left hand corner and insert a treasury tag or binding ring to keep them together and in order.

Mind mapping is another alternative to a full blown script, and is my favoured way of keeping on track.

This visual technique can take a little getting used to, but once mastered, has proven invaluable to many people.

Mind Mapping was developed by Englishman Tony Buzan back in the 1960's and has many uses other than presenting.

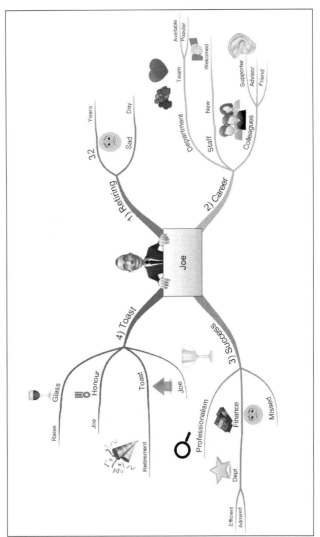

Mind map style script for a retirement speech

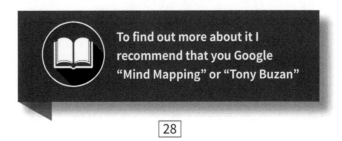

To find out more about it I
recommend that you Google
"Mind Mapping" or "Tony Buzan"

You can see an example of a mind map style script for a real retirement speech on the previous page. Typically mind maps have the topic in the centre and are read clockwise, starting at the one o'clock position.

You can download a larger, full colour, version of this example mind map from my website:
http://goo.gl/ZqocT0

Make it persuasive

The content of your presentation or speech needs to move your audience to take some action or to shift their opinion.

Having a basic understanding of human motivation is essential if you are going to write an effective speech. Don't worry, this isn't particularly complicated and you can get the gist in minutes. Here's the thing...

DON'T UNDERESTIMATE THE POWER OF EMOTION!

Data on it's own is not enough! Most people actually make their decisions based on emotional rather than logical reasons, and then look for data to validate that decision.

When I was a sales manager my new boss disputed this fact so I decided to challenge him.

I remembered that, earlier in the day, he had been telling us that his new company car would be a big beefy 4x4 rather than a traditional executive saloon. When I asked him why he had chosen this particular type of vehicle, he gave the following reasons:

"I'm the UK sales manager so I need a car that can handle all types of terrain" – *In truth he rarely drove any further than Birmingham!*

"Some parts of the UK get bad snow each winter and I don't want to risk getting stuck in a snow drift." – *In truth, living in the South of England as he did, the risk of getting stuck in a snow drift was minimal.*

When I said to him, "So it's not because it's a big macho car with a designer badge on the bonnet?", he went bright red and quickly changed the subject!

The third aspect of persuasion relies on whether the audience perceives the speaker as trustworthy or not. If your credibility is low, it's going to be much harder for you to give a persuasive speech.

Interestingly, the basis of persuasion was first written about by the Greek philosopher Aristotle way back in the 4th Century BC.

In his book, The Art of Rhetoric, Aristotle identified three distinct modes of persuasion.

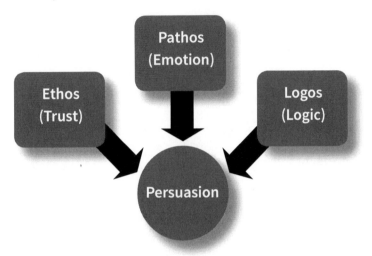

Ethos relates to convincing someone by building credibility and character of the speaker.

Many speakers rely on their Profession, Job Title and Qualifications to establish their credibility in the eyes of the audience.

Whilst they may be important, speakers should never underestimate the importance of non-verbal communication which can support or undermine an initially favourable perception.

Pathos relies on the creation of an emotional response to persuade the audience.

The most obvious examples of pathos in action are charity appeals which paint verbal pictures of starving children, maltreated animals or suffering families. I believe strongly that pathos has a place in most types of persuasive business presentation.

The two most powerful human drivers are pain and pleasure. In a business context these are more accurately reflected by the terms fear and excitement.

If you want to motivate an audience to change their opinion, the best way to do it is to choose content that hits each of these hot buttons.

For example:

- "Imagine how good you would feel if you were able to give a confident, professional presentation."

- "If we don't adapt to these marketplace changes quickly we will, in all likelihood, not have a company in 12 months time!"

- "How will you be able to afford to do all the things you want to do when you retire, when you haven't got a salary coming in every month?"

- "How will you feel when you are able to show your boss the huge savings that you achieved by switching suppliers?"

Logos is the final driver and relates to persuasion by logic and reason. When you know how to support an emotional case with a reasoned argument backed up by relevant factual data and case studies, your ability to persuade others will skyrocket.

CHAPTER 4 SUMMARY

Don't start with Power Point!

Always start by defining your outcome –
Think about what you want your audience to do after listening to your presentation.

Always tailor your presentation to suit your audience –
Remember, no two audiences are ever the same!

Write for the ear rather than the eye –
Read your script out loud and edit it so that it sounds good to the listener.

Condense your initial script into cue cards or a Mind Map –
It takes a lot of time and effort to memorise a script, and reading one out word for word will usually sound dull and boring.

Harness the incredible power of emotion –
Logic and data are rarely enough.

Chapter 5 – Valuable Visual Aids

"Slides should be an aid for the audience rather than a crutch for the presenter."

Now that you have your three act "script" you can finally think about adding in some visual aids. If you are using PowerPoint (or one of its equivalents), remember that audiences are turned off by speakers who put everything they are going to say on their slides, and then just read it out.

Do you need any slides at all?

Before you even consider producing any visual aids you should ask yourself, "Do I need them?" Some of the best, most memorable presentations and speeches never had any visual aids at all!

Perhaps we should start by considering for whose benefit the visual aids are being produced? Too many presenters create slides purely so that they can read them out in front of an audience like a script.

I am sure that you have experienced this type of presenter. How do you feel when they just stand and read out their slides without adding any extra value? Have you ever caught yourself thinking, "I can read you know!"

Design with the audience in mind

Your visual aids should be developed primarily for the benefit of the audience not the speaker. Their purpose is to reinforce, illustrate or clarify the presenter's verbal messages.

If your content will not benefit from any visual aids, don't waste time producing them!

Some presenters advocate abandoning the use of PowerPoint and its many alternatives altogether. While I have some sympathy with this approach, I feel that it is too drastic to be taken literally. Simple, well designed slides containing charts, graphs, or pictures rather than text can communicate certain types of information much more efficiently than words alone.

Images are processed by a different part of the brain than speech. If you are trying to convey something complex, a picture, chart or simple diagram can literally be worth a thousand words.

Sadly most people have never been taught how to build slides that actually add value to their talk. They just copy what their colleagues do and create bullet-point infested slides that are dense, wordy, and boring. The PowerPoint equivalent of a powerful sedative!

So let's look at how you can create slides that add value.

Avoiding 'Death by PowerPoint'

Many people blame PowerPoint (and its alternatives) for the boring nature of most business presentations, but we should always remember that PowerPoint is only a tool. It is neither good nor bad.

The real problem lies in the fact that most people do not know how to use it correctly. This, I believe, is because they have never seen it used well. They have learned by slavishly copying the boring, bullet-point riddled designs of their colleagues, and it is in this way that the poor use of PowerPoint is perpetuated.

A couple of years ago I was running an in-house pitching presentations course for a City PR company. When we came to the section on slide design, I asked them to show me their current slide deck.

True to form it was full text-heavy slides with multiple bullet points and few if any pictures. Every slide also featured the company logo in the bottom right-hand corner.

When I asked them why they designed their slides in this way, there was a long, uncomfortable silence. Finally, the MD replied "because that is what the customers expect." I pressed her further and she said, somewhat sheepishly, "because that's the way everybody else does it."

I then reminded them that their outcome, was to learn how to create presentations that clearly differentiated them from their competitors.

> "Suddenly they realised that, by delivering their messages using slides that were similar to everyone else's, they were shooting themselves in the foot."

Thankfully there is a better way. I want to inspire you to challenge the way slides are used in your organisation.

I dare you to become a PowerPoint pioneer! Follow these guidelines and set an example of best practice that will prove to your colleagues that there is a better way to use PowerPoint.

I hope you will have the courage and independence to take up this challenge, and in so doing improve the communication within your workplace.

Removing bullet-points makes your messages more memorable

The other scary bit of information is that traditional, text-dense, bullet-point riddled slides undermine rather than enhance the presenter's verbal messages.

Contrary to what most people think, the more text you have on your slides, the less your audience will remember.

Research by Dr Richard E Meyer, published in the book 'Multimedia Learning' (Cambridge University Press 2001), shows that eliminating bullet points leads to substantial increases in both recall and knowledge transfer.

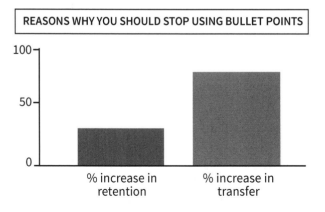

REASONS WHY YOU SHOULD STOP USING BULLET POINTS

Dr Meyer's research showed that the removal of bullet points produced a 28% increase in information recall and a 79% increase in knowledge transfer.

Note: In this study, knowledge transfer was defined as the listener's ability to apply the information they had absorbed to the "real world".

Dr Meyer's findings are echoed by more recent research published in 'Brain Rules' (Pear Press 2008). In it, John J. Medina, Director of the Brain Centre for Applied Learning Research at Seattle University, reinforces the benefits of replacing text and bullet points with carefully chosen images, charts and diagrams.

To see a fabulous example of how 'Brain Rules' will transform the way you design your slides, scan the QR code below to watch a SlideShare presentation by Garr Reynolds.

Just type the following link your browser or scan the QR code with your smartphone.
http://goo.gl/WtQ1a

The secret of effective slide design is to use simple slides with a narrative headline and supporting graphics. Slides like these are quickly absorbed, allowing the audience's attention to return to the presenter. Traditional, text heavy slides compete with the presenter for the audience's attention.

A few years ago I created a short video which summarises the key elements of intelligent slide design. I recommend that you check it out.

Just type the following link your browser or scan the QR code with your smartphone.
https://goo.gl/UtbweY

Here's what you should do to improve your slides:

1. Remove all unnecessary text
2. Stick to one clear idea per slide
3. Use simple, clear images, graphics or diagrams
4. Use photographs rather than clip art

 The late Steve Jobs, CEO of Apple, was a master of simple slide design. There are numerous recordings of his presentations on You Tube, which demonstrate the power of simple, clear slides. **https://goo.gl/0qQeFi**

TOP TIP!

Try the five-second test

If you are not sure whether your slides are too busy or not, try this little test. Show the slide to someone for only five seconds and then see how much they remember.

If they could take it all in, your slide is probably OK. If they couldn't, your slide is probably too complicated, so simplify it!

Remember the purpose of your slides is to support and reinforce your narrative, not repeat it verbatim!

 For more examples of these principles in action I suggest you take a look at Garr Reynolds' excellent book, 'Presentation Zen' (published by New Riders 2008).

Slides do not make good hand-outs

Presenters often justify the use of wordy slides by saying that they are designed to be printed out as hand-outs or posted on the intranet. While the sentiment is admirable, in practise it just doesn't work! Slides that try to be both visual aids and notes seldom do either job effectively.

Reading slides on a your computer, in silence, is very different from reading them as part of a live presentation with a speaker. In a live presentation, the audio narrative means that there is more competition for your attention, and so your slides need to be simpler.

If your slides can stand on their own, i.e. if a reader could make perfect sense of them without hearing you deliver them, then one of you is redundant, or soon will be…

Please note that I am not suggesting that you should not have a hand-out. I am just saying that a printout of your slides is not it! There are much better ways to create a useful hand-out, without compromising the effectiveness of your visual aids.

TOP TIP!

Use Notes Page View

The **"Notes Page View"** facility in PowerPoint allows you to create pages that have the graphic slide at the top and then text notes beneath it.

These notes can then be printed by selecting **Print** and then choosing the **Notes Pages** option from the **Print what:** *dropdown menu.*

This allows you to produce a visually attractive and useful presentation with clear supporting notes, all from within PowerPoint.

Alternatively, use your preferred word processor to produce a short text summary of the key points and supporting data, instead of printing off your slides.

To learn more about the Notes Page View feature in PowerPoint, enter the URL below into your browser or scan the QR code.

https://goo.gl/PlHvsT

You are a visual aid too!

Many people forget that they are their own best visual aid. You, the presenter, are a living, breathing audio-visual aid; much more powerful and persuasive than any piece of technology.

Don't be tempted to hide behind your slides. You are the one who can bring your content to life with stories, examples, passion and emotion.

Step forward, take centre stage and use your body language, eye contact and voice to engage your audience!

In the next chapter we are going to look at perhaps the most important part of your presentation: how you can make the most of your delivery.

CHAPTER 5 SUMMARY

Why are using slides?
The primary purpose for your slides is as an aid for the audience, not the speaker.

Use visual aids intelligently
If your content doesn't need a slide to clarify it or support it, don't use one.

Banish bullet points
Text dense, bullet-point driven slides cause the audience to remember less than they would have if you hadn't used them in the first place.

Keep your slides simple
Use the 5 second test to check.

Slides rarely make good handouts
Design your slides specifically to support your verbal delivery, and create a separate stand alone handout if required.

Chapter 6 – Dynamic Delivery Skills

"You cannot not communicate. Every behaviour is a form of communication."

Paul Watzlawick

No matter how well you have prepared, structured and designed your presentation, poor delivery can kill it stone dead in minutes.

I have seen boring subjects brought to life with a great delivery and I have also seen potentially exciting content reduced to dull, lifeless drivel by a poor delivery.

In the following chapters, you will discover a host of powerful techniques for ensuring that your presentation delivery is always engaging, entertaining and persuasive.

Before we explore these techniques, lets take a moment to consider the three main ways in which we communicate in more detail.

Understanding these will help you understand why the techniques in the following chapters are so important.

The Three Channels of Communication

In face-to-face presentations we communicate using three channels simultaneously:

- **Visual**
  Posture, Stance, Gesture, Facial Expression, Movement, Eye Contact
- **Vocal**
  Tone, Volume, Rhythm, Pace, Pauses, Intonation, Energy
- **Verbal**
  Language, Grammar, Words and Phrases

There is clear evidence that all three elements are essential, yet most average presenters spend the bulk of their precious preparation time focusing on the words. Perhaps that is one of the reasons why so many presentations are dull, boring and ineffective.

You will need to learn how to deliver those words effectively if you are to have any hope of convincing your audience to do what you want them to do.

In the following chapters, we are going to take a look at each in more depth. You will find each section packed with practical delivery tips that you can implement immediately.

I dare you to put them into practice!

THE POWER OF PRACTICE + FEEDBACK

The following chapters will cover everything you need to become an engaging and persuasive speaker there is one big caveat! Knowing these techniques isn't enough – you need to master them.

The Asaro people of Papua New Guinea have a wonderful way of expressing what I am trying to say.

> *"Knowledge is only a rumour until it's in the muscle."*

Regular practice combined with quality feedback is the fastest way I know of helping you master these valuable techniques.

Practice on its own is not enough
Contrary to the popular saying, practice doesn't make perfect, but it does make permanent. Habits are the result of repeated behaviours and if the behaviours you practice are bad ones, then they will become habitual. What you need is quality feedback to help you perfect and repeat the behaviours that will make you a better speaker.

What kind of feedback is best?
Like you, and most other people on our planet, I was brought up to believe that critical feedback was the most effective tool for helping others to improve. Thankfully, about twenty years ago. I discovered that this was nonsense.

The most powerful feedback is positive. and by that I mean the kind of feedback that focuses your attention on the things you are starting to do well and encourages you to do them even better. Feedback like this builds self-belief as well as capability.

At the beginning of every course, I explain that my feedback will be focused primarily on what they do well.

It has been my experience that shining a spotlight on desirable behaviours amplifies them.

> Once, after hearing this, one of the participants looked disturbed and said "but you will tell me what I am doing wrong won't you?"
>
> I replied, "Yes, if you really want me to, but, what do you think I will say?"
>
> She thought for a moment and said "You'll probably tell me that I pace around too much, that I speak too quickly, and that I have a habit of saying Um a lot."
>
> I replied "It sounds like you know this already and yet you have come on this course. How will my reinforcing it help you? Wouldn't you rather know what you are doing well and how you could do that more consistently?"
>
> She paused, and a big smile lit up her face as she nodded vigorously.

Where can I get quality positive feedback?

As this is a book and I don't know you and your circumstances personally, I can't be specific. I can however make some suggestions based on my own experience and that of my students. My advice is to seek out a mentor with the following qualities:

- Is an experienced presenter who is better than you currently are
- Is able to analyse your performance and provide specific feedback designed to build upon your existing strengths
- Understands that personal growth is about small, incremental improvements.

Such mentors can be found if you are prepared to look. They could be a boss or a colleague from your work. A professional presentation skills expert like me. A member of a Toastmasters International public speaking club, or a trusted friend or family member.

These recordings can be shared with your mentor electronically and then feedback can be given either face to face or by video call or email.

CHAPTER 6 SUMMARY

Speakers use three communication channels simultaneously:

- **The Verbal Channel**
  Words and vocabulary

- **The Vocal Channel**
  Volume, Pace, Tone, Intonation

- **The Visual Channel**
  Body Language, Facial Expression, Visual Aids

Make sure you give each channel the attention it deserves.

Practice makes permanent, not perfect.

Find a mentor if you are serious about improving your speaking skills.

Chapter 7 – The Visual Channel

In this section, we will look at how you can bring your content to life using your body language.

What do we mean by body language?

Body language or non-verbal communication includes behavioural aspects such as:

- Posture & stance
- Facial expression
- Eye contact
- Gestures
- Movement

When we watch others, we form an impression of their confidence, credibility and expertise based largely on these non-verbal elements. Experienced speakers understand which non-verbal elements effect their perceived credibility, and know how to manage these "cues" to be more persuasive.

Using "status cues" to increase credibility

Clearly, you want to project confidence and credibility, especially if you are trying to influence, persuade or lead your listeners. The study of your perceived credibility is known as "Status."

"Status cues" are specific behaviours that help you to raise or lower your perceived status in the eyes of your audience. I could write a whole book just on this topic alone, but here is a summary of the five most powerful ways to raise your status when presenting.

Stance

Adopting an open, upright stance with your shoulders back, your head up and your feet turned out just a little projects confidence and credibility.

Make sure your stance is balanced too, with your weight evenly distributed between both feet.

You don't need to stand like this all the time, but it is a great place to start and finish your presentation. It is also very powerful when delivering key messages, or answering questions.

Eye contact

Eye contact is one of the most powerful ways to create and maintain credibility.

In most cultures, eye contact is associated with honesty. If, for whatever reason, you do not make sufficient eye contact with everyone in your audience, they may not believe you. The key is to make and maintain an appropriate level of eye contact.

Most experts consider three seconds of continual eye contact to be ideal in a western, business context. While Some people find this remarkably easy to achieve, others find it a challenge. If you fall into the latter camp, you will need to practice until it becomes automatic and comfortable.

As well as helping you establish credibility, eye contact also provides a valuable source of feedback on how the audience is responding to your presentation.

TOP TIP!
Engage with everyone
When speaking to groups, it is important that everyone in the audience thinks that you are making eye contact with them. Mentally divide the audience seating area into zones (thirds often works well), and deliberately make eye contact with each zone throughout the presentation.

Head stillness

Keep your head as still as possible when making an important point or recommendation and your perceived authority will increase dramatically. Actors use this technique when playing powerful characters. Many teachers are taught this technique to help them maintain authority in the classroom.

Face touching

Habits like touching your face, rubbing your nose or playing with your hair tend to reduce your perceived authority and credibility.

Watching a video recording of yourself presenting is a great way to discover if you do any of these things!

If you do and you want to be more credible, I recommend that you make a deliberate effort to reduce these behaviours. Consciously channel this nervous energy into your voice, eyes and gestures instead.

Pace and pause

Although not strictly a non-verbal behaviour, it makes sense to include reference to this here as it also affects your perceived status. I will, however, cover it in more detail in the next chapter.

Speakers who speak slowly and clearly, and who are comfortable with deliberate pauses, are consistently perceived as having massive credibility.

If you are in any doubt about this, go to You Tube and search for recordings of well-respected orators like Barak Obama, Martin Luther King or Winston Churchill. Listen to their speed of delivery and use of pauses and you will see what I mean.

Making the most of the walk on

Inexperienced presenters often make the mistake of thinking that their presentation does not start until they start speaking. Nothing could be farther from the truth.

Your audience will start to make judgements about you as soon as you begin to walk-on. They will notice your dress, your walk, the amount of eye contact you make and your smile (or lack of it). Based on this information, they will instantly decide how interesting your presentation will be, even before you open your mouth.

You can increase your chances of creating a favourable first impression by planning and practising your walk-on in advance.

Walk on confidently, smile and make eye contact with your audience. Before you start to speak, pause for a second or two, engage with your audience silently through eye contact. As you do this, imagine that you are inviting them to join you in a safe, comfortable and familiar space for the next few minutes.

A strong, confident walk-on will also help you settle your nerves. If you adopt the physiology of confidence, the mind will quickly calm down, and both you and your audience will start to expect an enjoyable experience.

Using gestures – What do I do with my hands?
The appropriate use of gestures can add energy, emphasis and drama to your story. Many novice presenters, however, worry overmuch about their gestures. They seek to curb them by clasping their hands together or putting them in their pockets.

Instead, just allow them to hang loosely by your sides when not gesturing. Alternatively, you can rest your fingertips together, lightly, at waist level, but do not interlock your fingers. Leave your hands free to gesture naturally.

Interestingly, new research seems to suggest a link between gesturing and verbal fluency. Trying to suppress gestures unnecessarily may have a detrimental effect on your ability to speak naturally.

Remember that gesturing is normal. You should relax and allow it to flow naturally. You only need to take action if you have developed any irritating gesture habits.

Typical distracting gestures include:
• Flapping your arms up and down in time with your speech,
• Wringing your hands
• Recurrent face touching
• Playing with pens

TOP TIP!
Get yourself filmed
If you are not sure if your gestures are irritating or annoying, seek objective feedback. Ask a friend or colleague to record your presentation. Most smart-phones can record high quality video so you don't have a valid excuse not to.

Should I choreograph my gestures?

Adding some specific gestures can help emphasise your messages and bring your topic to life. I wouldn't get too worried about this for the moment as I will cover this in more detail in a later bite-sized book.

If you do want to experiment, here are some of the different gesture types you could use.

Rapport gestures

Open, bilateral gestures are seen as inclusive and help you to build rapport with your audience

Descriptive gestures

Gestures like finger counting or drawing out a shape with your hands help your audience to visualise parts of your content.

Directional gestures

Monolateral gestures like holding out one hand to one side of your body and then later the other hand on the other side help the audience to separate ideas and concepts.

Sincerity Gesture

Touching your chest with one hand whilst talking about something you care about emphasises your personal investment in the topic.

Emphasis gestures

Pointing, punching the air or hitting a palm with the other fist all add emphasis to your verbal messages.

Size gestures

The spacing between your hands or your fingers can be used to indicate things like a small problem or a big opportunity.

Near/Far gestures

These gestures can help shift your client's time perspective by supporting verbal messages like – "I know these changes seem a long way away, but if we don't start to prepare now, they will be on us before we know it."

Movement? – Make it purposeful

I often get asked whether it is a good idea to move around while presenting or better to stand still.

Opinions on this topic have changed over the years, and today it is perfectly acceptable, and indeed more natural, to move around a little during a presentation.

Where you move to and how much you move, will depend on a number of factors including the space available, the room layout and the audience size.

The most important thing is to make sure your movement is purposeful. Random fidgeting or nervous pacing is distracting, and should be avoided. Video feedback can provide valuable insight here.

In particular, I recommend that you avoid:
- Pacing backwards and forwards
- Rocking from side to side
- Dancing on the spot

I will be writing another bite-sized book about "stagecraft" in the coming year and will address this subject in much greater depth, but here are a few simple suggestions to get you started.

Try location anchoring

You can help your audience follow the flow of your speech by linking specific parts of your speech to specific areas of the floor.

Imagine that you are talking about your organisation and that your presentation has three main sections. The first is a little bit about the history and origins of the company.

The second is an explanation of what the organisation is like today. And the third is a teaser about some of the exciting future developments you have planned.

Many presenters use location anchoring to signpost the structure of their speech during their introduction, and in so doing help make the speech more interesting and memorable.

In your introduction, you could move to a spot on the right hand of the speaking area (as you look out at your audience). From here you can explain that you will start with the history or your company.

Next, move to the centre of the stage, and as you do so, tell them how you will be talking about the present-day situation.

Finally, as you walk to the left of the stage, you can tell them that you will be finishing with a glimpse of the future.

You have now set up three location anchors and associated them with different parts of your speech. As you move from one anchor spot to another during the remainder of your speech, your audience will automatically know that the focus is shifting between past, present, and future, without you having to say anything.

If you have slides, use a remote 'clicker'

Many presenters unconsciously restrict their ability to move around the speaking space because they insist on using the keyboard on their laptop to control their slides. This is crazy!

There are now many different types of affordable wireless remote control that are compatible with PowerPoint and Keynote. These consist of a USB receiver that plugs into any laptop, and a small, handheld, remote that allows you to do simple things like advance your slides and blank your screen.

Buy a simple remote   **TOP TIP!**
There are many different models, and some of them have all sorts of added functionality. Beware! The more buttons on the remote, the more likely it is that you will press the wrong one and blow your credibility.

At the time of writing, I use a Kensington Wireless Presenter with built in laser pointer. These are available from Amazon for less than £25 and are very reliable and simple to use.

http://amzn.to/2ie3H43

CHAPTER 7 SUMMARY

Start with a confident posture
Feet hip-width apart, toes pointing very slightly out, weight equally distributed across both feet.

Your presentation starts before you say a word
Walk on with confidence and make eye contact *before* you start to speak.

Natural gestures help you to speak more fluently
Don't worry too much about your gestures unless they are distracting.

Move around with purpose
Replace nervous fidgeting and pacing with purposeful movement.

Break away from your laptop
If you are using PowerPoint, use a simple remote control.

Chapter 8 – The Vocal Channel

Learn to use your full vocal range

Presenters who speak in a monotone, with little variation in tone, volume and emphasis have the uncanny ability to send their audiences into a deep trance.

To be sure that you avoid this you will need to give some thought to how you use your voice.

Good vocal variety brings a presentation to life.

The human voice box is capable of creating an astonishing range from a barely audible whisper to a thunderous shout. Sadly, many presenters get stuck in a vocal comfort zone and so use a tiny fraction of their vocal capability.

This leads to a dull monotonous delivery style that is better suited to putting people to sleep rather than waking them up!

Effective presenters understand that their voice is one of their most important tools, and so they spend time learning how to use it to best effect.

There are many different elements to voice work, but I recommend that you focus on just three initially:

• Power
• Pace
• Placement.

Power

By power, I mean specifically your speech volume i.e. how quietly or loudly you speak.

The human voice is capable of speaking at any volume between a whisper and an ear splitting scream, but as I mentioned earlier, most people only use a small part of this vocal range. Speak too softly for too long and your audience will struggle to hear you. Speak too loudly for too long and they will feel overwhelmed.

However, when you can consciously vary your volume to suit your message, you can keep them entertained and enthralled.

To develop your abilities in this area I recommend that you try the following activities:

- Ask for honest feedback on your current volume and vocal variety
- Have someone record your speech along with that of others and then compare them objectively for audibility.
- Experiment with reading out a passage of text or a poem at different volumes ranging from very quiet to very loud. Ask a friend or family member to listen to you and to challenge you to go even quieter or even louder.

Remember, a louder voice adds emphasis and urgency. A quieter voice draws the audience in, and creates the effect that you are sharing an intimate secret with them.

Pace

By pace, I mean how quickly you speak. My research has shown that most people are unaware of their speaking speed.

In conversation, English speakers typically speak at around 170-180 words per minute. When speaking to an audience, as a presenter, a pace of 120-130 words per minute is much more effective. If you don't believe me, just listen to some of the great speeches from orators like Winston Churchill, Barak Obama and Steve Jobs.

A helpful metaphor

One of my clients had developed the habit of speaking very fast when he presented. He took a big breath at the beginning and then spoke continuously until he ran out of breath. The result was that his audience had no time to take in what he was saying.

Public speaking, I explained, is a bit like feeding your audience. You want them to ingest and then digest the most they can.

When you speak fast, it feels like you are trying to force a whole loaf of bread down our throats in one go. We feel overwhelmed and we don't have the chance to asbsorb most of what you are saying.

If you want us to get the maximum value from your speech, you'll need to divide the 'loaf' into a series of bite-sized pieces. If you feed these to us, one bit at a time, and give us time to chew and swallow it before giving us the next piece, your presentations will be much more effective.

TOP TIP!

Experiment with your speaking speed

1. Print out a passage of text containing exactly 120 words.
2. Record yourself reading this passage aloud while timing yourself.
3. Now practice reading the same words at different speeds so you can get used to how it feels to speak more slowly and deliberately. Remember to record these experiments.
4. Play back the recordings, listening for the effect that slowing down or speeding has. Speaking faster creates excitement and energy. Speaking slower adds seriousness and authority. By varying the speed of your delivery appropriately you can affect the audience's perception of your messages.

Placement

By placement, I am referring to the location in your body where your voice is resonating. The depth and pitch of your voice can improve your perceived credibility and authority. It is possible to adjust your tonality by becoming more aware of whereabouts in your body your voice is resonating. For example – your nasal sinuses, throat, chest or belly.

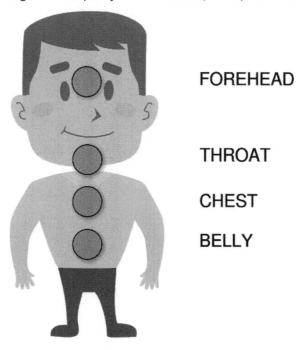

FOREHEAD

THROAT

CHEST

BELLY

Practice Your Placement

One of the easiest and quickest ways to experiment with changing your speaking pitch is to speak out loud while imagining that your voice is coming from a particular area of your body.

Speaking from your "forehead" produces a higher pitched, thinner tone that carries less weight with the audience.

Speaking from your "throat" produces a slightly deeper, more authoritative tone.

Speaking from the "centre of your chest" produces an even deeper, more resonant sound.

If you struggle with vocal variety, consider getting some training from a voice coach. It doesn't have to be expensive, and it can be one of the best investments you make. You can probably find one locally with a quick internet search.

The Power of the Pause

> *"It's the space between the notes that makes the music.*
> *It's the space between the walls that gives the room its size.*
> *It's the space between the words that gives your talk its depth."*
>
> Richard Wilkins

Don't be afraid of silence - it is one of the most powerful but most underused speaking skills. It sounds so easy but many people find it a challenge. When you start out, a couple of seconds of silence can feel like an eternity but, with a little practice, you'll find that you soon get used to it.

Silence adds impact and gravitas to your speaking and has the added benefit of giving your audience time to think about what you are saying.

Professional speaker Brian Tracy suggests that there are four distinct types of pause.

- **Sense pause**
- **Dramatic pause**
- **Emphatic pause**
- **Sentence-completion pause**

The **sense pause** allows your audience time to absorb new information. The **dramatic pause** helps to make your point stick in the audience's mind. The **emphatic pause** highlights the importance of a point

Finally, the **sentence-completion pause** is a popular technique used by professional speakers to create audience interaction and engagement.

The speaker says the first part of a well-known saying or line and then pauses to allow the audience to finish it.

For example:

- Beanz Meanz...(Heinz)
- An apple a day.... (Keeps the doctor away)
- They think it's all over... (It is now!)

There are many benefits to learning how to hold a pause including:

- It buys you time to recall what you are going to say next
- It gives your listeners time to think about what you said and to make connections with their existing knowledge or experience
- It boosts your perceived credibility and gives you more authority in the eyes of your audience

Practice pausing

Ask a question and then hold the silence for 8-10 seconds and notice the effect it has. Your audience will fill the gap with that most valuable of all commodities –thinking!

If you find holding a pause difficult, try counting silently inside your head.

This simple technique gives your brain something to do and stops you saying something. You can start with a slow count of five to begin with and then increase it as your comfort zone grows.

CHAPTER 8 SUMMARY

How you say it is at least as important as what you say.
Learning how to you use all the different variables within your voice is a key element of becoming a persuasive presenter.

Three key vocal elements are –

- Power (Volume)
- Pace (Delivery speed)
- Placement (Pitch & resonance)

Learn to use more vocal variety.
Your voice is capable of an enormous range. Persuasive present-ers continually work on expanding their vocal comfort zone to become better speakers.

Chapter 9 – The Verbal Channel

CHOOSE YOUR WORDS WITH CARE

So far we have concentrated on the visual and vocal channels and now, finally, we are going to touch on the words. Before we do so, I'd like to remind you that the words are only a part of communication. The best-crafted script is useless if the non-verbal and vocal delivery is poor.

Common verbal errors

The three most common verbal mistakes that I see presenters make are:

- Too much content
- Use of inappropriate jargon
- Use of unnecessary filler words

Awareness is the key to change, so seek feedback if you are unsure whether you have a habit of falling into any of these traps. If you have, follow the guidelines below to eliminate them.

Too much content

Less is more when it comes to effective presentations and speeches. Learning to edit your speech, and leave out interesting but non-essential content, is a key skill. Calculate the number of words you need to suit your time slot, based on a maximum speaking speed of 130 words per minute.

A lesson from the London Olympic Bid

A few years ago, I read a fascinating article by Lloyd Bracey, the voice coach for the successful London 2012 Olympic bid. In it he explained how he worked with each of the members of the bid presentation team. Timing was a critical element as they would be cut off if they went over time. To avoid this, they rehearsed their speeches repeatedly, editing and re-editing until each was perfect.

"When Craig rose to speak, I knew that every word and every image in that presentation had earned its place."

Learn how to edit your content

It's hard to resist the temptation to keep adding more and more information to your presentation but it is essential that you do resist.

Survey after survey has shown that audiences are turned off by presenters who overload them with too much information.

You need to consider what you want to achieve and how much time you have. The shorter the speaking time you have the more ruthless you need to be with your editing.

Just as in the Olympic bid example above, you need to make sure that every piece of data, case study or example is necessary and relevant.

> Once, on an advanced presentation skills course, I was asked to prepare and deliver a seven-minute speech.
>
> Later the same day, the tutor asked me to edit the original speech and deliver the same key messages in only half the time!
>
> Finally, I was challenged to condense the same speech even further, and to cut it down to just 1.5 minutes.
>
> It was a tough exercise, but it made me think about which bits of my speech were essential, and which weren't.

However much time you have for your presentation, I encourage you to ask yourself the following question.

"If I only had one minute to make my case, what would I say?"

This will help you get clear about what your core message is. Then, and only then, can you assess whether the rest of the information in your speech supports or detracts from that message.

Eliminate unexplained jargon and acronyms

Every profession has its own specialised set of vocabulary, abbreviations and acronyms. These forms of verbal shorthand can facilitate communication between professionals "in the know" but they are also the cause of much misunderstanding.

Listeners are often too embarrassed to seek clarification for fear of being ridiculed, so they either switch off or make inaccurate assumptions. As a presenter, you must take responsibility for the language you use.

The solution

Avoid using jargon wherever possible and only when it is necessary. If you have to use jargon, make sure that you explain it clearly. Don't fall into the trap of presuming that everyone in your audience will understand: they probably won't, but they'll be too polite (or scared) to tell you. Acronyms are a useful shorthand but only if your audience understands them.

Banish unnecessary or irritating filler words

Many people are unaware that they have developed the bad habit of adding unnecessary filler words when they pause for thought. Um's, errs or filler words such as 'like' or 'actually', add nothing to your messages.

Whilst the occasional one isn't a disaster, repeated use will quickly start to irritate and distract your audience.

When I was a student I had a physics lecturer who had the annoying habit of saying "Do you see? Do you agree?" At the end of almost every sentence.

After his first lecture, my fellow students started taking bets on how many times he would use this phrase in his next lecture. Because we were listening out for his "catch phrase" we completely failed to pay attention to the content of his lecture!

Are you prone to the use of annoying filler words?

The truth is you probably will never know unless:

a) You ask for feedback from your friends, family or colleagues

b) You get someone to record your presentations and then have the courage to play back the recordings listening out for these unnecessary verbal distractions.

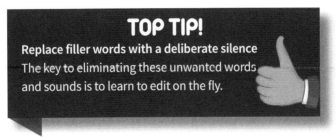

TOP TIP!

Replace filler words with a deliberate silence
The key to eliminating these unwanted words and sounds is to learn to edit on the fly.

Slow down, think before you speak, and catch yourself before you say the filler word or sound.

"Less is more"

Robert Browning

CHAPTER 9 SUMMARY

Less is more.
Don't overload your audience with too many messages and too much information.

Be careful with jargon
Beware of using jargon, abbreviations and acronyms unless you are 100% sure that your audience will understand.

Replace unnecessary filler words with a silent pause.
Over use of filler words like um; err; actually; and sort of; will undermine your credibility.

Chapter 10 – Rehearsal Strategies

Always make time to rehearse your presentations, especially your opening and your conclusion.

The more important the presentation, the more time you should devote to rehearsal.

An Olympic athlete would never turn up for the games without having spent years training and practicing their chosen event so why is it that way too many presenters "crash and burn" primarily because they failed to prepare properly for their big moment in the spotlight?

I know you'll probably be thinking, *"I don't have time to rehearse."* But is this true or is it just an excuse?

Think about it! Everyone in the world has the same amount of time, they just make different decisions about how they spend it. If you are serious about becoming a better speaker, then you should commit to doing everything it takes to give your best performance, and that most definitely means practicing every presentation.

Thankfully there are a range of different rehearsal techniques at your disposal, some of which take very little time!

- Rehearse in front of an audience
- Rehearse at home on your own
- Rehearse in your head

Combine these techniques for maximum affect!

Rehearse with an Audience

The ideal way to rehearse an important presentation is to practice out loud to a group of colleagues who have been forewarned that you want them to give you specific, constructive feedback afterwards.

Nothing beats a run through in front of a live audience. But it does take a bit of time and effort to set up, but don't let that put you off.

Many of my clients tell me that it was easier to organise than they thought. Most people like to help others and feel flattered to be asked to give feedback to a colleague.

Benefits:

- You get a realistic idea of how much time your presentation or speech will take to deliver
- You get objective feedback on both the content and the delivery, allowing you to make any necessary changes before you deliver it "for real"
- It allows you to practice handling questions and helps you to prepare for any unanticipated ones
- By demonstrating the importance and value of this type of "run through" you encourage others to do the same
- Allows you to practice and get feedback on non-verbal aspects of the presentation such as body language, eye contact, gestures, movement and vocal variety

To get better, more specific feedback, you may find *it helpful to download and print off copies of my* *presentation assessment sheet using the link or QR code* **https://goo.gl/cGgGVM**

Rehearse aloud on your own

Practicing in front of an audience isn't always practical so remember that you can still practice on your own at home or at work.

Alternatively, try presenting out loud to a mirror, so that you can see your expressions as you speak.

TOP TIP!

Imagine your audience in front of you

Make the most of your solo rehearsal by visualising your audience . Practice speaking to them, making eye contact with them and moving around purposefully.

Benefits:

- You can use your smartphone to record and time your speech for review purposes
- By reading it aloud you can spot any clunky sentences or difficult-to-say word combinations, and amend them
- Solo rehearsals are easy to set up and repeat, allowing you to become more familiar with both the content and flow of your presentation

In addition to these two powerful practice strategies I also strongly recommend that you also use the following mental rehearsal technique.

Rehearse in your head

Many people know and accept that athletes use mental rehearsal as part of their training regime. Sadly, most don't make the connection with presenting.

I've talked to many professional speakers, and most, if not all, visualise themselves presenting at their best to improve their "on stage" performance.

Mental rehearsal can be done anywhere, without disturbing other people. It also takes less time because in your imagination, you can "compress time" and thereby mentally rehearse the key elements of your presentation in a couple of minutes or less.

The key is to visualise yourself giving the presentation perfectly. After all, I very much doubt that the Olympic sprint champion, Usain Bolt, repeatedly imagines himself getting beaten when he is training.

Warning!

From my own extensive experience coaching thousands of speakers, I know that many nervous presenters mentally rehearse, but most are not consciously aware that they are doing it.

They make the mistake of visualising failure rather than success. They relive all their faults, recall their worst presentations and vividly imagine themselves giving a poor presentation. Is it any wonder that they feel nervous or anxious, with all of that going on inside their heads?

Remember, like the best athletes, the best presenters mentally rehearse success.

Visualise from three perspectives

I recommend that you run through your presentation in your mind's eye from three different perspectives. I use this exercise when working 1:1 with my clients.

I ask them to stand in a different spot for each position and then to describe what they are hearing, seeing and feeling.

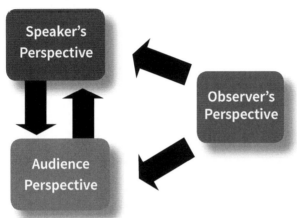

1. **The audience's perspective**
   In your mind's eye imagine sitting in the audience. See yourself, as the presenter, walk on confidently and deliver your presentation. Visualise yourself performing at your very best. Describe how you look, how you stand and, how you sound when you are at your very best.

2. **The presenter's perspective**
   Now imagine that you are the speaker. You are in your body, looking out through your own eyes. Notice how you feel and sound as you present magnificently. Describe what you see as you look out and notice your audience responding positively to your messages.

3. **A neutral observer's perspective**
   Finally, imagine you a neutral observer or coach. Watch yourself presenting through the eye of the observer and see what you notice now. What is the you who is presenting doing well? What improvements, if any, would you suggest to help the "other you" be even better?

Visit your local Toastmasters Club

Many of my clients tell me that have difficulty finding a safe, supportive place to practice their speaking skills. That is when I tell them about Toastmasters International.

Don't let the name put you off, it's nothing to do with red coats and weddings. Toastmasters International is a global not-for-profit network of friendly and supportive public speaking clubs.

The best way to find out if joining a Toastmasters club is for you is to visit a local club and see for yourself. There's no charge for visitors and you are guaranteed a warm welcome.

I've been a member of Toastmasters for more than ten years, and I still learn something at every meeting.

Find out more by visiting www.toastmasters.org

CHAPTER 9 SUMMARY

Practice, practice, practice
If you're serious about becoming a better presenter you must make time to rehearse.

Create opportunities to practice in front of a "safe" audience
The more important your presentation is, the more reason you have for rehearsing it in front of an audience.

Solo rehearsals
Practicing aloud on your own will help you learn your material and iron out any glitches before you do it for real in front of others.

Rehearse in your head
World class presenters, like top athletes, rehearse their presentations in their mind's eye, seeing, hearing and feeling themselves presenting at their very best.

Chapter 11 – Managing Nerves

"Everyone gets butterflies in their stomach before an important presentation, the trick is to teach them to fly in formation."

Anon

It's natural to be nervous

You may think that you are the only person in the world who gets anxious or panicky at the thought of speaking in public, but you're not! Even the most experienced speakers get a little edgy before they speak.

If you care about your presentation and your audience, it would be inhuman not to feel anything. The challenge is not to eliminate your nerves but to reduce their negative effects by transforming them into a source of positive energy that brings your delivery to life.

The two faces of confidence

Confidence is a funny phenomenon. It's not something you can buy in a shop or hold in your hand, it's a feeling you have about yourself, or a label you give other people.

Judging confidence in others

Have you ever seen someone else presenting and thought that they were confident? How did you know?

Unless you're a mind reader, you can't know for sure what they were thinking or how they were feeling. You made a judgement call that they were confident based on several observable behaviours.

Typically, the kinds of behaviours that we associate with confidence include a combination of:
• Looking relaxed
• Smiling
• Making eye contact easily
• Speaking slowly and clearly

- Using pauses and looking comfortable when doing so
- Moving purposively

This means that other people may believe that you are a confident speaker even though you think that you are not.

Self-confidence

Our assessment of our self-confidence is subjective and often differs wildly from how other people perceive us.

It's based on many things including:
- Our upbringing
- Our recollections of good and bad past experiences
- The feedback we received from others (particularly in our formative years)
- A tendency to focus on our shortcomings and ignore our strengths

How to rebuild low self-confidence

This is the subject of a whole book on its own and believe me, there are plenty of them out there! As this is a bite-sized book, I'll cut to the chase and give you some useful ideas to get you started.

Choose to change

Set the intention to let go of your past and change your limiting self-perceptions. Personal change starts with a decision. Start a confidence journal and write in it regularly. Here are some suggestions for the type of things to capture.

Positive reference experiences

Reflect on times when you have displayed self-confidence in any context and recall them in as much detail as you can. It could be at work, on holiday or with your family or friends. Ask other people you trust for examples of when they think that you have demonstrated confidence.

Your successes

I find that many people have developed the habit of focusing on their failures. They are their own worst critic. They will obsess on the fact that they forgot one tiny bit of their speech and ignore the fact that they got 90% of it spot on.

To break this insidious habit, you need to force yourself to look at the other side of the coin. Every day, set aside five minutes to jot down some things you did well. You'll find this a challenge at first but, like me, you'll find that it gets easier and easier, the more you do it. You can download a couple of helpful worksheets and confidence building activities from the Presenters Edge website. Just type this link into your browser or scan the QR code with your phone.

http://goo.gl/AC6RM8

Tips for overcoming nerves

- **Be prepared!** – Allow enough time to plan your presentation and be clear about what you are going to say and why you are saying it
- **Rehearse!** Practice makes perfect. The more important your presentation, the more you should make time to rehearse
- **Reframe the feelings.** Instead of labelling them as nerves, think of them as a sign of excitement and anticipation. The physical symptoms are much the same
- **Breathe from your belly.** When we get nervous we tend to stop breathing properly and this just makes our nerves worse. Deliberately take a couple of deep breaths from your abdomen before you start to speak. This will calm your nerves and ensure that you have enough air to speak clearly
- **Act as if you were feeling confident.** Even though you may be feeling a bit nervous to begin with, take on the posture and expression of someone who looks confident and in control. If you act as if you are confident, you will start to feel more confident. Stand tall, relax and put a smile on your face
- **Pause before you start to speak**, make eye contact with your audience, smile and imagine that you are inviting them into your world for the duration of your presentation
- **Imagine** sucking in all the nervous energy that is leaking out through fidgeting and channel it back into your voice, eye contact and gestures
- **Question** any negative thoughts about your ability or right to present and replace them with more realistic thoughts. Remember, your audience wants you to do well

73

CHAPTER 11 SUMMARY

It's normal to be nervous
I've yet to meet a presenter who can honestly say they don't get a few butterflies before speaking in public.

Face up to your fear
What you are afraid of is extremely unlikely to happen so face it head on and you'll see it start to shrink.

Focus on the audience, not yourself
Paying attention to your audience takes your attention away from yourself and your nerves will subside.

Fake it until you make it
Behave as if you were confident and your audience will think that you are confident.

Become aware of your strengths as well as your weaknesses
Seek out constructive feedback on your existing speaking skills as well as your areas for improvement.

Chapter 12 – Audience Interaction

Hands up if you enjoy being lectured to?

I didn't think so, so why is it that so many public speakers fall into the trap of conducting a monologue with their audience? When challenged about audience interaction many speakers use one or more of the following excuses to justify their approach.

- Not enough time for two-way interaction
- Fear of losing control
- Worried about not being able to respond to questions appropriately
- Scared of the audience
- Don't know the best ways to get audience interaction

Relax, interacting with your audience is much easier than it seems. In the next few pages I'll share the techniques that I and other professional speakers use to involve our audience.

Proven audience engagement tips

Start by setting the intention to engage your listeners

Engagement starts with your desire to engage. Set aside your fears about grabbing and holding your audience's attention. They are nothing compared the damage you do to your credibility if you don't even try.

Understand the different levels of engagement

In simple terms, engagement is when the people listening to your presentation do something because of something you say or do. This could be an **external action** such as raising a hand, clapping, nodding; or an **internal action** such as agreeing, becoming more curious, empathising or feeling an emotional reaction to your message and its delivery.

Here are a few ideas to get you started

Ask for a physical action

If you are speaking to a large group, or if time is short, there probably won't be a chance to get much verbal interaction. However, asking a simple question and requesting a raised arm in response, can work very well.

The trick is to make sure you choose your question with care. Pick one that you are confident most people in the audience will respond positively to e.g. "Raise your hands if you are attending this course voluntarily" Alternatively, if you are feeling brave you can do things like asking people to stand up and stretch, or even shake hands with the person next to them.

Example

I was once standing for election for an international post in a voluntary organisation. Each candidate had to give a 5-minute speech to 2000+ people in a packed convention centre and I was drawn to speak after 14 of my 24 fellow candidates.

As my turn approached I could see that the audience were getting increasingly bored and restless. With 5 minutes to go, I decided to tear up my prepared speech and do something different.

When my turn came, I walked out on stage and started by asking everyone in the audience to stand up and stretch. They did! And the energy in the room was raised dramatically.

I then asked them to sit down UNLESS they had been a local club president. Some sat down. I then asked those who remained standing to sit down UNLESS they had held a national office. More people sat down.

I continued this questioning process until only myself and a few other people were still standing, thus demonstrating my extensive experience in the organisation in an interactive and engaging way.

Share a personal story – be real

Stories are memorable, especially ones that have a personal connection. Sharing your fear or excitement will engage your audience. It's also a lot easier to come across as genuine if you are speaking honestly about something you care deeply about .

Welcome questions from your audience

Many presenters take questions reluctantly because they worry that an audience member will ask a question to which they don't know the answer. I find it incredibly useful to think of questions, not as threats, but as gifts. They are an opportunity to:

a. test the audience's current reaction to the topic

b. clear up any misunderstandings quickly

c. give more relevant information.

You can find out more about handling questions in Chapter 13.

Encourage open discussion

Getting your audience to discuss and debate a topic can be a great way to generate significant interaction but how you do it depends on the time available. In a training environment, it is common to have either whole group discussions or to split the audience up into smaller discussion groups. (I call these *Buzz Groups* because of the buzz of discussion and energy they create.)

TOP TIP!

Getting discussion, and keeping control of it

When you have a large audience with a theatre style room layout can be challenging. Here's a technique that works very well in this setting.

Ask people to turn to the person next to them, and discuss or share their answers to a relevant question e.g. "What benefits could this new approach bring to your team?"

Give them 1 minute each and time it rigorously. Then call their attention back with a bell, whistle or hooter. Now, if you have time, invite a few people to share one idea or opinion, from the discussion, with the whole group.

These are just a few tried and tested ways to get you started. If you want more inspiration, check out my blog where I regularly post articles on this and other presentation skills-related topics. www.inter-activ.co.uk/gavins-blog

In conclusion

Try out these audience engagement ideas for yourself and see what happens. I know that you will be pleasantly surprised.

CHAPTER 12 SUMMARY

Think of your presentation as a two-way communication.
It's easy to assume that a presentation is one sided but it's vital that you get your audience doing something even if it's just thinking.

Get your audience to move.
This is particularly true if they have been sitting still for any significant length of time.

Ask them questions.
Questions engage you audience and get them thinking.

Get them to discuss something

Encourage them to ask questions of you.
If necessary, have a couple of questions prepared to get the ball rolling.

Chapter 13 – Handling Questions

I have noticed that many speakers dread the traditional Q&A slot at the end of their presentation. When I ask them why this is, the most common reasons given are:

- Fear of losing control
- Fear of being asked difficult questions
- Fear of not knowing the right answers
- Fear of making a fool of themselves
- Fear of nobody asking any questions

In this chapter, I'll address all these concerns and share with you some simple techniques that will help you to turn this ordeal into a powerful part of your presentation.

The importance of questions

Audience questions play an important part in most educational or informative types of presentation and it benefits both the audience and the presenter.

Audience benefits

It gives the audience the opportunity to clarify anything that they are uncertain of, check their understanding and raise any concerns.

Presenter benefits

It gives the presenter a chance to assess the audience's level of understanding and "buy in", correct any misunderstandings, clarify and expand on points that are of particular importance to the audience.

Anticipate likely questions

It's true that you can never anticipate every question, but that's no excuse for not preparing for the most likely ones. Adopting an ostrich mentality by burying your head in the sand is a sure-fire recipe for failure. Grab a piece of paper and a pen and think about your audience. If you were them, what would you want to know? What information would you need? What concerns or fears would you have? If possible, ask other people too.

When I was a young marketing assistant with Esso Chemicals, I attended an international meeting. At it, I and each of my opposite numbers from across Europe, had to give a five-minute progress report on the implementation of a new piece of software in our country.

When my German colleague came up to speak, we all noted that he had many more slides than were normal, but he didn't use many of them.

Afterwards we descended on him and asked "Why all the slides?" Looking slightly puzzled, he simply responded "In case anyone asks the questions!"

Clearly he had tried to anticipate every possible question and had prepared a slide to answer each one, if it came up!

How to get more questions

It's not always the presenter that is afraid of a Q&A session. Audience members too, often feel reluctant to ask a question because they feel:

- Under pressure to come up with a "good" question
- Scared in case their question is seen as "stupid" by the presenter or their peers
- Embarrassed to admit that they didn't understand something the presenter said

These emotions lead to that uncomfortable tumbleweed moment when the presenter asks "Are there any questions" and is greeted with a wall of silence.

As the presenter, it's your job to do everything you can to prevent this. Here are some tips that I use.

Encourage questions in your opening

During my introduction piece, I usually include a few words about questions. I talk about their value and I tell my audience that, in my book, there is no such thing as a stupid question.

I also acknowledge how most people are afraid to ask questions for fear of looking stupid. I explain that there is in fact nothing to fear. If they don't understand something there will almost certainly be others in the room who don't understand it either but who are too afraid to ask. When you ask a question, you are helping others as well as yourself.

Make the questioner feel OK
Another great way to encourage more questions is to "big up" the first people to ask a question.

Using a phrase like "What a fabulous question" makes the questioner feel validated and sends the message to everyone else that questions are genuinely welcomed here.

Techniques for handling questions
When faced with a question there are various ways you can respond depending on your desired outcome. Let's look at a few options and think about how and where you could use them.

Answer directly
This is the most obvious response, if you know the answer that is. You just answer the questions as clearly and directly as you can and then ask the questioner if that answered their question. If you don't know the answer, say so and offer to find out and get back to the questioner after the presentation.

Seek clarification
It's quite common to be asked an unclear or ambiguous question and you may be tempted to answer based on your own assumption of what the questioner meant. When this happens, I would encourage you to resist the temptation to answer and instead seek clarification before responding. This signals that you genuinely want to understand their question or concern, and it also buys you more thinking time.

Return to sender
As its name suggests, this is where you ask the questioner to answer their own question or give their own opinion before you respond. It works particularly well when you have a "sniper" in the audience" who is deliberately asking difficult or controversial questions. "It sounds like you have an answer, would you care to share it with us."

Ricochet/redirect
Sometimes it's appropriate to redirect the question to someone else in the room who has experience or expertise in that area. If you are going

to use this one, try to give the person you are redirecting to, some warning so that they can gather their thoughts. E.g. "That's a great question Duncan, (pause) Now I know that James has been working on that area for some time now. James, could you perhaps share your thoughts in reply to Duncan's question about..."

Open the question up to the whole audience

Sometimes it may suit your purpose better not to answer the question yourself, but to open it up to the audience. This is particularly true when your objective is to educate your audience and to get them thinking.

When you do this, don't be surprised if you don't get an immediate response. As previously mentioned, your audience may initially be afraid to respond. The temptation to answer your own question will be strong, but you must resist it. If you stay silent and wait, someone will usually respond.

Defer answering until later

Sometimes you may be faced with a question that is best handled outside of the presentation situation. This is often the case if it is a very specialist question that requires a complex answer that is only of interest to one or two people in your audience. Explain that time is limited and that, as the question will take some time to answer, you would be happy to meet the person after the presentation to discuss it face to face.

When to take questions?

Choosing the most appropriate time to take questions can be critical to the success of your presentation.

In general, there are three opportunities to allow questions:

- Anytime during the presentation.
- At set intervals.
- At the end.

Let's consider each one in more detail and think about when and where to use them.

Taking questions anytime

This is where you encourage your audience to interrupt you whenever they have a question. It is most commonly used in longer training courses or workshop settings.

Pros:

- **Instant answers.**
  Allows you to answer questions and clarify points as soon they arise.
- **Encourages interaction.**
  Creates lots of opportunities for interaction between you and your audience, making the presentation feel more like a dialogue than a monologue.
- **Boosts credibility.**
  Showing a willingness to take questions at any time makes you appear much more confident and credible.

Cons:

- **Interrupts flow.**
  Being stopped in mid flow by a questioner can throw nervous presenters off their train of thought.
- **Interrupts timing.**
  Getting repeatedly side-tracked to answer tangential questions can cause you to run out of time or overrun.
- **Potential loss of control.**
  Taking questions during your presentation means that you risk losing control of the content and direction.
- **May annoy others.**
  As well as causing you to digress from your stated topic, taking too many questions can annoy other audience members who want to progress at a faster pace.

Questions at set intervals

As its name suggests, this is where you only take questions at set points during your speech. It is typically used in workshop or training situations, which have clearly delineated modules. Questions are typically taken at the end of each section.

Pros:

- **Gives the presenter more control.**
  Allowing questions only at specific times allows the presenter to retain control of the agenda and helps them keep to time.
- **Checks understanding before progressing.**
  Taking questions at the end of each section allows you to check that your audience have reached the desired level of understanding before you move on to the next topic.

Cons:

- **Could affect timing.**
  Unless you allow sufficient time in your programme for questions, you can still find yourself running out of time if you get a lively and curious group.
- **People may forget their question.**
  The more infrequent the Q&A sessions, the greater the likelihood that important questions will be forgotten and that the opportunity to address them will be lost.

Questions only at the end

Many speakers prefer this option because it gives them the maximum control. It works well for shorter speeches but in my opinion it has significant drawbacks

Pros

- **Continuity & Control.**
  With no risk of interruption, you can deliver your prepared speech without overrunning (assuming you have prepared and rehearsed it beforehand!)
- **Questions may have been already answered.**
  You may have successfully anticipated the most common audience questions and built the answers into your presentation.

Cons:

- **Important questions are often forgotten.**
  Any delay in being able to ask a question increases the chances that the questioner will forget their question by the time they are allowed to ask it.
  While this may seem like a "get out of jail free" card to many

speakers, it means that important questions often remain unasked and therefore unanswered.

- **Can result in a loss of audience engagement.**
When an audience member has a question or concern which they cannot get cleared up then and there, they may make a decision to "switch off"

Question Management Tips
- Tell the audience when they can ask questions
- Don't allow questions to dominate the presentation
- Expect questions and prepare answers
- Listen carefully to the question and give yourself time to compose your response before replying
- If necessary, repeat the question to make sure **everyone** in the audience has heard it, before responding
- When you do answer, make sure that your reply takes in the whole group, but make special eye contact with the questioner, and check back with them at the end
- Give positive answers or follow up a negative response with a positive alternative. "That's right it doesn't do that; however, it can do ..."
- If you don't know the answer to a question, don't guess or waffle. Either ask for help from another member of the team or make a note to get an answer to the questioner afterwards

When conducting team presentations, the person answering the question should ideally be the person who covered that point in the presentation.

Remember most people don't ask questions to catch you out. They genuinely want to understand what you are saying.

CHAPTER 13 SUMMARY

Learn to look forward to the Q&A
Think of audience questions as a gift rather than a threat.

Pause before answering
Not only does this give you more thinking time, it also boosts the perceived credibility of your answer.

Be prepared
Expect questions and prepare answers in advance, especially for those difficult to answer questions that fear most.

Chapter 14 – Let's Recap

They say that repetition is the mother of learning so,with the aim of reinforcing my key messages, here is a recap of the main points in this book. Implement any of these ideas and I guarantee that you will become a much more persuasive presenter.

1. **Plan backwards**
   The first thing you should do when you start to write a new presentation or speech is to ask yourself "what is my outcome? What do I want my audience to be thinking, feeling and doing at the end of the presentation?" Knowing the answer to this question will allow you to plan backwards from that end point and design a persuasive presentation that will deliver your desired result.

2. **Establish the relevance up front**
   WIFFM is an acronym for "What's in It for Me?" If your audience cannot immediately see the relevance of your presentation, and how it will benefit them, they are likely to switch off. I believe it is essential that you should establish the relevance of your content early in the presentation!

3. **Use a simple three act structure**
   Every effective presentation needs to have a clear structure that is easy to follow and makes sense to the audience. It needs to have a beginning that hooks their attention and establishes relevance. It needs to have a middle that makes your case and creates emotional as well as logical engagement. Finally, it needs a compelling conclusion with a clear call to action.

4. **Eliminate bullet points in slides**
   Slides are an aid for the audience, not a crutch for the presenter. Always prepare your slides **AFTER** you have written your script. Focus on visuals rather than text, e.g. graphs, flow charts, pictures and diagrams. Remember that research shows that the use of bullet points in slides **reduces** the amount people remember, so remove them from your slides wherever possible.

5. **Learn to use your body language**

   Your presentation starts as soon as you take the stage or the audience start to look at you. The way you walk on sets their expectation level and the way you walk off determines their final impression. Treat these phases as equally important parts of your presentation. Experiment with using 'Status Cues' to enhance your credibility and confidence.

6. **Learn to use your vocal variety**

   Your voice adds light and shade to your presentation. Sadly, most people use only a fraction of their vocal range. Practice and, if necessary, seek assistance from a voice coach to make sure you use your vocal range for emphasis and to maintain interest. A monotone simply won't do.

7. **Learn to use the power of the pause**

   Pauses and silences are powerful tools for adding emphasis, increasing credibility and allowing your audience time to process and digest your key messages. Learning to hold a deliberate pause takes practice, but will enhance your credibility.

Over to you

Capitalise now it is up to you to take what you have learned and put it into action. I am confident that when you do, your confidence will blossom, your effectiveness will sky-rocket and your career will benefit.

If you choose not to, that is OK too. Maybe it is just not the right time for you. However, I suggest that you keep this book handy and dip into it again when the time is right.

Tell me what you think

As you will probably have discovered by now, I am passionate about the value of feedback. I would be delighted to receive any comments and suggestions regarding my writing, via my website.

If you have noticed any mistakes of an editorial nature, please accept my sincere apologies. If you let me know what they are, I will fix them in future editions.

Best Wishes

Gavin Meikle

The Presentation Doctor

Portsmouth. UK

August 2016

You can leave your feedback online via our convenient feedback page
http://goo.gl/H2kXcC

Reading List and Useful Links

Presentation Delivery

Be Heard Now
Lee Glickstein – Broadway Books

Presenting to Win
Jerry Weismann – Prentice Hall

Never Be Boring Again
Doug Stevenson – Cornelia Press

Presentation Design

Beyond Bullet Points
Cliff Atkinson – Microsoft Press

Presentation Zen
Garr Reynolds – New Riders

Resonate
Nancy Duarte – Wiley

Websites

TED Talks – www.ted.com Riveting talks by remarkable people

Slideshare – www.slideshare.net Examples of good (and bad) slide decks

The Reluctant Presenter – www.inter-activ.co.uk/gavins-blog
Presentation tips blog

About the author

Gavin Meikle is the **Presentation Doctor** and has been helping transform nervous and reluctant presenters into confident communicators for more than twenty years. A Scot by birth, Gavin is now is based in Portsmouth, England where he runs his own communication skills consultancy.

A Presentation Coach and a Speech writer
Gavin is unusual in that he loves writing as well as speaking and this additional skill means that he is well placed to help his clients find the right words to express their messages.

A Presentation Skills Blogger
Gavin also writes a popular blog on presentation, communication and influencing skills. It's full of useful tips, ideas and examples and is regularly updated.
www.inter-activ.co.uk/gavins-blog

An Online Learning Course Creator

Gavin is developing a range of easily accessible online presentation and influencing skills courses. To find out more, visit his online courses web page.
http://goo.gl/Ldv7rY

Gavin is available for:
- 1:1 presentation skills coaching
- In-house training programme design and delivery
- Conference speaking, facilitation and emcee assignments

www.inter-activ.co.uk

Printed in Poland
by Amazon Fulfillment
Poland Sp. z o.o., Wrocław